Narcissism in relationships

How to recognize a narcissist, detach yourself from him and finally become happy

Annika Pütz

CONTENT

What you can expect in this book.......................1

Narcissus - The Beautiful.........................3

When the scales tip - personal style or disorder?......6

Narcissism and Co-Narcissism - The "Dream Team 9

Charming and irresistible! 13

Narcissism in Social Media 13

The Date - Recognizing Narcissism...................14

Psychoterror - The love that destroys your life. 20

A loving relationship with a narcissist - is it possible? 27

What can you do about your partner's narcissism? 29

The separation - My world is in shambles.............31

Why is breaking up with a narcissist worse than any other before?...............................31

You are not to blame !............................37

A healthy self-worth is poison for every narcissist.42

What is wrong with me and others?...................42

They are great! - Strengthen self-confidence 47

Overcome crises - preserve happiness.................51

What you can expect in this book

I feel sick, tired and old. I have no more energy for anything. I am just waiting. Waiting for a kind word, waiting for him to get back to me, waiting to be acknowledged. I can't understand what I'm doing wrong, it's not good for me, I know that. But I can't help it, I stay. It's my own fault. I just have to try harder, become more tolerant. Then everything will be fine."

Everyone who has had one or more relationships or encounters with a narcissist has had such thoughts. Very often we encounter this topic when choosing a partner. Have you been disappointed repeatedly, do you feel used or even guilty?

Surely a friend has already reported back to you that you keep "falling for" the same type of man. Perhaps you are already thinking about this on your own and are considering fundamentally revising your "prey pattern". Possibly you are still in such a relationship and have the desire to free yourself from it, but do not know whether you really see "clearly"?

This is exactly the topic we are dealing with in this book. I want to help you become aware of the characteristics of narcissism and invite you to reflect on what behavior patterns have led you to repeatedly encounter narcissistic men. I also want to offer you guidance on how to break free from destructive relationships.

For the sake of simplicity, I am writing from the point of view of a woman. At this point, however, it should be said that narcissism naturally also exists among women. This differs in some respects from the characteristics of narcissism in men, but in the end makes little difference. In principle, therefore, men who repeatedly encounter narcissistic female personalities are also invited to reflect and break destructive behavior patterns.

Narcissus - The Beautiful

Narcissus was the common child of the river god Kephisos and the water nymph Leiriope. He was born out of rape and grew up to be a young man filled with pride in his own beauty. Boys and girls alike idolized him, but he heartlessly rejected them all.

The young Ameinias also experienced this rejection. Narcissus sent him a sword. He could not cope with this insult and killed himself with the sword, but not without first calling upon the gods to avenge him. Nemesis or Aphrodite heard his plea and punished Narcissus with insatiable self-love.

When he looked at himself in the water, he fell madly in love with his reflection, without realizing that it was he himself whom he saw in the water. This love was characterized by unfulfillability, he recognized this, but it was of no use to him. He pined for his reflection until his death.

Pausanias, a Greek travel writer, related that Narcissus sat down by the lake one day to enjoy his reflection. A leaf fell into the water and distorted his reflection. Narcissus, shocked and believing he was ugly, then died. After his death, he was transformed into a daffodil.

The term "narcissism" has developed from this Greek mythology. Roughly summarized, this describes personalities who often appear demanding, arrogant and arrogant. These are apparently very self-confident people, or at least they actively convey this image to the outside world. Behind this external effect, however, there is often a rather weak, easily hurt self-esteem, which makes it difficult for these people to deal with criticism. Even more - narcissists forgive criticism only with difficulty. No one is supposed to recognize how sensitive and weak the person behind the facade actually is.

The problems of narcissists start early. They do

not live up to their own standards, are driven by perfectionism and plagued by fears of failure. They often have problems at their workplace and never do themselves justice.

When the scales tip - personal style or disorder?

What constitutes our personality is a complex question. We all have parts of impulsiveness, volatility, dramatization, egoism and many more in us. Each person has a different way of perceiving their environment and interacting with others. The distribution and expression of our annidual characteristics or our patterns of thought and action allows us to develop a personality. It is shaped by our external world and significantly by our experiences in childhood and adolescence. In general, these characteristics balance each other out, even if some characteristics are somewhat more pronounced and others less so.

We move from a personality to a personality style when some character traits appear more clearly than others. Thereby the transitions are to be considered fluently. Most people are thus rather a "smorgasbord" of different personality styles, which are more or less pronounced.

But when do we speak of a "disorder" of a personality style? This is always the case when certain characteristics are overly pronounced and at the same time prove to be very inflexible. If the way of thinking and feeling stands out strongly from the environment and has a decisive effect on the behavior of the person , this can indicate a disorder. However, it is difficult to judge from what point we speak of a very pronounced, dominant personality style or a disorder. The transitions between the two variants are fluid.

Disturbances in interaction behavior are most apparent. This can have a negative impact on friendships, acquaintances or family relationships. This is due to the distorted perception of reality. For example, neutral actions are perceived as above average negative or events are perceived very exaggerated. However, people with a disorder not only perceive their environment differently, but also themselves. In this way, achievements can be portrayed in an exaggeratedly positive way.

In order to obtain a clear diagnosis, a visit to a psychiatrist or therapist is essential. In psychotherapy, a diagnosis can then first be made with the help of "psychoeducation" and a suitable form of therapy can be sought together. For this purpose, many individual discussions are necessary. This form of treatment, however, requires a certain insight on the part of the person affected and a strong relationship of mutual trust between patient and therapist.

Based on this problematic and very difficult to make diagnosis, in the further course we will speak only of personality styles.

Next to the narcissistic one, the so-called "borderline personality style" is the best known and is known to most people. In modern psychology this personality style is called "emotionally unstable". It is characterized by a clear tendency to act unexpectedly and without consideration of consequences. Affected persons tend to have strong mood swings, which can result in sudden outbursts of anger or sometimes even violent actions. They are not sure of themselves, their preferences and needs and therefore often feel empty. They often make disproportionate efforts to avoid being abandoned. This often leads to self-injurious behavior and even suicidal thoughts.

Another quite well-known personality style is the "dependent" or also "dependent" one. Affected individuals like other people in their lives to make the decisions, even prompt them to do so. They often ask others for advice and have their decisions reaffirmed. What is striking is that people with this personality style subordinate themselves to the needs of people with whom there is a dependency. Those affected are very compliant and rarely demand anything. They do this because they are very afraid of being alone. They then experience themselves as helpless and feel unable to take care of themselves. The worst thing for them would be to be abandoned by their partner, friends or relatives.

NARCISSISM AND CO-NARCIS-SISM - THE "DREAM TEAM

I have presented to you exactly these two styles not without reason. Just like yin and yang, the dependent and, in some cases, the emotionally unstable style form a unit with narcissism. Thereby, a bilateral disorder does not always have to be directly present. Strongly pronounced parts are already sufficient here to find each other "attractive".

When taking a closer look at a relationship between a narcissist and a dependent person, one speaks of co-narcissism or also of complementary narcissism. Here a mutual satisfaction of both worlds of needs takes place. The characteristics of a co-narcissist are comparable to those of a dependent person.

They are overly concerned with making their partner happy. Their own needs are pushed into the background. The need for tenderness, love and attention is simply too overpowering and makes everything else seem unimportant. Narcissists have a talent for conveying the feeling of uniqueness very early and at the beginning of a relationship. Finally, the co-narcissist has found someone who sees what is special in one. The fear of never finding such a person and remaining alone forever is deeply rooted in them. Only too glad to "take care" of someone at last, lay the world at their feet.

A narcissist gladly accepts this. After all, he feels most comfortable when he is met with admiration by others, because that shows him that he has successfully disguised his own feelings of inferiority. Perfect at first sight! If it weren't for the fact that it is difficult to please a narcissistically inclined person:

"S. planned a weekend together in the mountains. It should be a surprise for her partner P.. He always works very long hours during the week, is often stressed from work. P. reacts dismissively to her announcement, tells her that he has important things to do, but goes along anyway. Arriving at the hotel, P. is critical of the room furnishings. While still unpacking his suitcase, he emphasizes that he wants to leave early the next morning because he has other appointments. S. feels guilty for not having paid sufficient attention to P.'s needs. She firmly resolves to make more of an effort next time."

The example of S. clearly shows how co-narcissists think and feel. They do not give any space to their own disappointment about their partner's reaction and take his reaction as an opportunity to reconsider the supposed misbehavior on their part.

Here, however, the lack of empathy also becomes visible. A narcissist's thoughts mainly revolve around himself. The fact that S. might not want to return so early the next morning or the question of what plans she has do not play a role for him.

The circle of friends of an addict is also under

great strain. Often, the addict has no choice but to reveal his suffering to his circle of friends sooner or later. But the closest confidants are made very difficult and not infrequently their objective feedback falls on deaf ears. The co-narcissist quickly gets into the position of wanting to defend the partner. Too present in these moments are the beautiful moments of the relationship, which the narcissist gives her in homeopathic doses. The guilty conscience of not being grateful enough for them is too great.

Charming and irresistible!

NARCISSISM IN SOCIAL MEDIA

Facebook, Instagram, Tinder, Twitter, etc. The platforms are as diverse as the target groups. Each format offers plenty of room for selfies. The competition is fierce, so that for most of us, skills to that end have become a matter of course in dealing with social media. As these skills grow, so does narcissism in our society.

"Photos without filters?! No way!" is the first thing many people think. If we honestly ask ourselves what the reasons for our activity on these platforms are, many will notice narcissistic traits in themselves.

"More beautiful, better, more extraordinary" is the motto here, under which we place our self-promotional profiles. The photo of our food gives the impression of sophistication, the vacation photo shows a certain level of financial security and photograph a building without you in the foreground? In this context, however, make all these memories are less for us to remember beautiful vacations, moments with friends or extraordinary moments.

Rather, it is deeply embedded in the back of our minds to tell the whole world how cool, popular and exotic we are. But do we have a choice? Only those who get out their narcissistic parts and seriously deal with their self-marketing have a chance of standing out in the thicket of social media in the long run. The pressure to stand out from apparent competitors is great and makes us get creative.

THE DATE - RECOGNIZING NARCISSISM

The desire for security, trust and family makes many singles become sentimental and develop the longing to share all this with a man. Profession, age, studies, circumstances of the place of residence or even increased demands and other obligations make it difficult for us to find a suitable partner.

The first step out of single life is therefore often online dating. A few years ago, this was still a taboo subject, but nowadays it's completely normal, even taken for granted. Countless dating apps and Internet portals are available to us, some of which are free, but most of which are paid.

Caution is advised! Narcissists are only too happy to cavort on the World Wide Web, because here they have the opportunity to exploit their full potential. Nowhere else is it so easy to meet a flirt partner.

But how do you recognize a narcissist? They are hard to see through, they are masterful at being able to adapt to every woman, every situation and every need. When something is too good to be true, your "alarm bells" should go off. "Love Bombing" is the keyword here. Especially at the beginning of a relationship, this term refers to a state in which you are showered with compliments, promises, attention and affection.

Narcissists are adept at emotionally manipulating their victims. The more emotionally starved you are, the more receptive you are to their advances.

The urge to find the perfect partner, analogous to your romance novels, is great. In order to stand out from said competition on the World Wide Web and to highlight our individuality, we often tend to reveal too much personal information about ourselves.

For example, information about your age in combination with your marital status says a lot about you. For example, there is a good chance that a woman who is 38 years old and childless has a deep desire to finally start a family. The photo of your dog conveys that you are very fond of animals.

Narcissists are usually very intelligent, attractive and care about their appearance. They know how to respond to you compassionately and emphatically. AND - they do their research! They use above mentioned information, maybe you can be found on other portals like Facebook. Skillfully, they subtly ask you about your preferences, fears and hopes. The goal is to quickly create a deep attachment. In this way, the narcissist becomes exactly the man you have always been looking for.

If you have found a man who appeals to them in the social networks or on dating platforms, then a personal date will not be long in coming. Many men are charming and courteous, but not every one of them is immediately a narcissist.

However, a narcissist will always cross your personal boundaries. Very quickly, he will try to get close to you sexually, again unnoticed subtly. This can be the glass of wine too much, which prevents him from driving home late in the evening. How convenient it would be then if he could spend the night at your place, after all you don't want any inconvenience at the beginning of their romance because he has to laboriously pick up his car the next day. He will then either take you completely by surprise or go on and on under the pretext of just wanting to hold you a little in his arms. All this, however, he does not do without affirming again and again that it would actually go against his principles or that it would be the first time that he would do "something like that".

There is a method to this approach of **rushing intimacy**.

He will quickly call you his girlfriend and bombard you with exaggerated ideas about the future. The words "I love you" will also not be long in coming. Flattered and relieved in the belief that you have finally found the man for life, who wants to be with you firmly, who has the same interests as you and gives you all the security you have always wanted, you are trapped. Faster than you think, you are dependent on him.

But! You can test him. For example, if he asks you about your favorite movie or song, make something up. Possibly he will answer with enthusiasm that it is also his favorite movie. Basically, listen to your gut feeling. If something seems funny to you, there's a good chance that it really is. And if something seems too good to be true, it probably isn't.

But there are other "warning signals" and these often come from his environment. Partnerships that have fallen apart? That can and has happened to each and every one of us. Nevertheless, if he tells you about his many relationships that have all dramatically gone down the drain and he rejects any blame, you should be careful.

You may have already dated him a few times and so slowly he starts to criticize you and your personal preferences and characteristics. Often he starts with your appearance: too much makeup here, too little there. It may also happen that he insults you in public. Set limits for him! Let him know that he has crossed a line and will have to behave differently in the future. A narcissist will not be able to handle this, he will either get angry or ignore you for days.

It takes a lot of experience to recognize a narcissistic man. Most of the time you will not succeed at first sight, but perhaps with a little practice at second sight.

In summary, here are some traits that may indicate that you are sitting across from a narcissist during a date:

• Narcissists are usually highly intelligent, which is why we often find them in leadership positions.

• As mentioned at the beginning, narcissists often have difficult interpersonal relationships, so they usually have few "real" friends.

• He will do everything to be a dream man for you. This is done by sharing all your interests, feelings and perceptions. In short, he will tell you everything you want to hear ("love bombing").

• The first date seems artificial, staged. Everything is just "a bit too much".

• He will be more charming than average towards you, it is important to him that you feel very special.

• You will always get the impression that his statements are not true, more it will be the touch of a feeling to which you may not pay enough attention.

• Proving a narcissist's lies is difficult, so listen to your gut.

• Narcissists are very ambivalent, they say one thing and then do something completely different.

• He is never at fault, he has you for that.

PSYCHOTERROR - THE LOVE THAT DESTROYS YOUR LIFE

"S. is sitting with P. in his favorite restaurant. He looks deeply into her eyes while he talks about how happy he is to have found S.. He had never felt such a deep friendship for anyone as he did for her. Until now, all women had left him, he had been deeply hurt and could not look at a woman for a very long time, until... yes, until he met her. He now finally feels he can heal again. But for now it can only be a friendship, because he is not yet ready for a relationship. Affected, he looks to the side and tells her that he is sad to have met her so late. He talks haltingly about his last relationship, in which he invested everything he could. He even took her to a counseling center, but it was no use; she became more and more depressed and cared less and less for him, even though he sacrificed himself. She would not have had sex with him anymore either, he was left alone by her with his needs and would have had to be content with himself."

A typical case of **"love bombing"**, one of the many manipulation techniques that narcissists use to lure you into dependence and keep you there. As already described, this technique is used especially at the beginning of a relationship to lure you into dependence. At the same time, when you read through it a second or even third time, you will notice what P. is actually saying. The person in his hormonal frenzy will at first be enchanted by his openness, his vulnerability and finally also by his realization that she is something very special. But what P. is really saying there is that his ex-life partner is depressed and that he "only" wants a friendship.

Narcissists are driven by the insatiable urge to be admired and respected. Therefore, it is not uncommon that a woman is not enough for them and they have affairs. But the narcissist has provided the reason from the beginning: He only wants a friendship. So what can you counter in this regard?

One part of love bombing is **"future faking**. This can be compared to the half-life of election promises. A narcissist very quickly recognizes the unfulfilled needs of his counterpart and makes promises, forges realistic and also unrealistic plans for the future. This tactic serves to maintain interpersonal relationships, loosely based on the motto: "Nice to keep in line."

Another method is **"gaslighting"**. This is a technique in which your partner convinces you of untruths with great matter-of-factness, so that you cannot question them at all. Even more, the narcissist will actively change circumstances and make you know that everything is the same as before. This can be, for example, the key that you always put on the table. The narcissist will put it on the dresser and tell you with an incredulous expression that the key is always there after all. You will feel increasingly insecure, almost crazy, and naturally dependent on him.

Before he can succeed in this method, however, the narcissist must be absolutely sure that you trust him blindly.

"Silent Treatment" is used especially by narcissistic personalities. Through this technique, the addict is made to submit to the wishes of the narcissist. In the process, you are made to feel insecure with silence. This is to make you realize that you have reacted wrongly. For example, you disagree with him. As a result, he starts to be silent. This unsettles you, but a narcissist remains firm; after all, you are supposed to be given time to think about your misbehavior. The more you probe, because the situation is almost unbearable for you, the longer this state will last.

You have spent magical dates together, passionate nights with him and suddenly there is nothing? No call, no text message, no explanation. He's just gone and doesn't get back to you. Every minute you look at your phone, but no explanation arrives. If you've experienced something like this, it's called **"ghosting."** This pattern of behavior is very common in today's age of dating apps. The large selection of "dateable" people is enormous, so who wants to commit to one person right away? Increasing inability to commit and the growing shyness about conflicts also move people to this behavior.

But how this affects those affected is not considered. Ghosting can leave a strong sense of insecurity. People with such personality styles, who are attributed with a fear of abandonment, may experience a crisis as a result. The further development of ghosting or the related form is **"benching"**. In this case, the narcissist simply does not contact you at all, but rather promotes you to the "bench". He often does not contact you for a few days and then suddenly reappears in your life. In this way he plays with the addict's fears of loss and binds him more and more to himself.

Triangulation" is often used to create jealousy. It is meant to destabilize and belittle the partner. A good example of such behavior is the "misdirected" text message or email to another woman or even the ex-wife confirming that they had dinner together. When asked about this, he will very credibly affirm how sorry he is.

Such behavior does not fail to have its effect. The dependent person becomes insecure, feels rejected, and will redouble efforts to get the narcissist because of his jealousy.

Another widespread approach, from which sufferers have to suffer a lot, is called **"Blame shifting"**. With this method, you will never get it right. A narcissist can skillfully transform himself from perpetrator to victim. He evades responsibility for his misconduct by simply shifting the blame onto you. He cheats? But only because you put him under pressure with your desire to have children. You find out that he is flirting with other women on his cell phone? It is your fault if you "snoop" on his cell phone.

This method makes sufferers despair. They have no chance to fight against it. Systematically you are taught: "You are wrong, your narcissistic partner is ok." Until you believe it yourself. This tactic transitions almost fluidly into **"victim blaming."** Here, the perpetrator-victim relationship is pulled to yet another level entirely. This can also be observed quite wonderfully in our example. There, P. exclusively describes how he felt, how he "sacrificed" himself. What he did this with remains withheld from us. The question why the ex-wife had been so depressed also remains unanswered here. Instead, he stigmatizes her very strongly as the perpetrator.

If you have been in such a relationship for a longer period of time, it may also have happened to you that you felt the need to keep a log of your conversations with your partner or to have the tape run directly along. You are increasingly wondering if something is wrong with you and you should seriously question your sanity. I can tell you: you are not "crazy"! This is the method of **"crazy making"**. The narcissistic partner first says one thing and later something completely different, but insists that he never said anything else. Although you know very well that this is not the truth, he will persuade you with a vehemence and persuasiveness to the contrary until you believe him more than yourself.

It happens the same way with shared memories. A narcissist who likes to resort to this method will gladly reproduce your memories completely differently than you experienced them. This doesn't mean little things like the color of the park bench or whether the weather was cloudless or cloudy, but rather basic memories, like the beautiful experience at the fountain in the park or at the ice cream parlor downtown. This twisting of memories is a particularly toxic tactic to unsettle you and keep you attached to him. The narcissist also likes to increase his negative influence by having a strikingly bad memory and not even remembering beautiful moments that are important to you, such as the heart that carved you into a tree back then. In this case, you will not only be insecure, but also deeply hurt.

If you have ever been in a relationship with a narcissist, you may have recognized one or more methods. Realizing that you are in perfectly normal mental health will help you break free from such connections. Often the tactics flow into each other without transition and are hard to tell apart.

The goal is always the same in the end: Through accusations, hurtful remarks, dishonesty, evasion, blaming, forgetting, reproaching, he wants to hurt and humiliate you. Finally, he does not need to pay attention to your feelings, because you are to be left alone, traumatized and sad. He waits for you to come back to him, full of panic at being left alone, begging for forgiveness.

There are many different reasons why women end up in narcissistic relationships. It can be your personal life crisis, your lack of self-confidence, or even long relationships in which you were bored with the habit. A charming, smart man who showers you with compliments can be very tempting.

A LOVING RELATIONSHIP WITH A NARCISSIST - IS IT POSSIBLE?

When we meet a narcissist, when we succumb to his charm and believe his many compliments, our first impulse would be YES! But now we know some of the narcissist's methods and that he thrives on fooling you. We now know that he has a hard time taking your feelings into consideration and the bottom line is: a narcissist is not able to form a caring and loving interpersonal bond to build a healthy relationship! Such a relationship is characterized by the emotio-nal dependence of the partner. A loving relationship is possible only if both partners meet on eye level and with mutual respect. But if you don't have this respect, you can have a relationship with a narcissist.

If you are involved with such a man, sooner or later you may be confronted with his affairs. You must realize that his constant hunger for admiration will drive him to it. It is hard to imagine that you alone can give him all the recognition he needs. His lack of empathy will not allow him to feel guilty. Also, you have to live with the fact that he will always try to make you jealous. Dexterity is required when dealing with such situations. Do not go further into it, but do not make fun of it either and meet him with a certain seriousness. Because a misbehavior on your part may have the result of making a "scene" for him.

If you absolutely want such a man to stay with you and you are determined to have a relationship with him, you simply have to show regularly that you are very afraid of losing him. The more humble and submissive you are and the more he can do whatever he wants with you, the more he needs you. You will probably have to get used to his affairs, but it cannot become dangerous for you.

You should not try to restrict such a person too much. Leave him alone if he is busy with his cell phone and listen away if he receives strange calls. Perhaps he will also stay out a night or two on flimsy grounds. Instead, take care of the household and thus "have his back".

It will often happen to them that he comes home in a bad mood because something again did not go as he imagined at work. Be patient. Tell him how well he does his work and that no one can hold a candle to him anyway. That will be balm for his soul.

Get used to the fact that he will never see

everything you do for him. But he will notice that you let him do what he wants, that you don't restrict him and, above all, that you don't "bitch". Do not overwhelm him with your own wishes, but show him admiration and appreciation. As long as he believes that you are happy to be at his side, he will not leave your side.

In the end, if you put up with his behavior and accept him as he is, if you understand that he just can't help it, then you will suffer as little as possible from your relationship! But does that make you happy?

WHAT CAN YOU DO ABOUT YOUR PARTNER'S NARCISSISM?

It is very difficult to convince a narcissist that his behavior is not good for you. He simply will not understand or realize it. Healthy reflective behavior would require that there be some capacity for empathy. Furthermore, such a man will not admit his faults, because that would mean that his true self would come out. He would have to show you how vulnerable he is, what fears he has and what shortcomings he possesses. But this is out of the question for a narcissist, for him it is most important to keep up appearances. Convincing him of this is an almost hopeless struggle.

At this point it should be mentioned again that a narcissist definitely suffers from himself. The constant pressure to maintain the perfect external image means a lot of stress. He is constantly driven by the fear of "blowing his cover". The constant thirst for recognition can be understood like a defective battery. He cannot store the admiration he so desperately needs. Thus, such a man is driven by the constant search for it. Often these people fall into depression due to more or less minor things. Perhaps there is a deep desire for help, but the step is often too big. Among all diagnosed personality disorders, the narcissist is most often driven by suicidal thoughts, which can easily end in actual suicide.

The separation - My world is in shambles

WHY IS BREAKING UP WITH A NARCISSIST WORSE THAN ANY OTHER BEFORE?

A separation and especially the separation from a narcissistic man can be very difficult and requires good preparation. Expect that he will reproach you, because a narcissist must always be right. That being said, why is this exact relationship ending worse than any other? What is behind this dynamic? In most cases, a breakup is never pretty. Finding a good closure in the process is a natural need for an adult love relationship. In the best case scenario, both partners will have some conversations and see the matter for what it is: the relationship had ups and downs and both had their parts in the failure.

In a narcissistic relationship, however, the partner is innocent. Even more, the reason for the breakup is borne solely by the partner. In addition, his ego was hurt, because he has no shortcomings, at least officially.

However, it makes a difference whether he separates from you or you from him. If he separates from you, the rejection will be hard for you. It is hardly to be expected that he will have an adult conversation with you and take your feelings into account. The parting will be hard, short and painless for the narcissist.

At least he will show you his painlessness, because this will not pass him by without a trace either. He just doesn't care how you feel. But why does he end the relationship when he is actually suffering from it? Probably you will have simply become too close to him. Narcissists are not capable of truly committed relationships. They quickly feel constricted and controlled by you. Another reason can be, then you are too complicated for him. He wants to subdue you quickly and make you compliant. If he only succeeds with difficulty, he will soon distance himself from you.

For you as a dependent co-narcissist, a world will collapse. From one day to the next, you face your greatest fears. You are alone and feel confirmed in the thought that no one loves you. Even if this painful state looks like the end of the world to you at first, it is the best thing that can happen to you in such a relationship. After all, he will leave you alone. He has probably already found a new woman who is easier for him to control and who flatters his ego better.

This state of pain is worse than any before because you simply feel confirmed in everything bad you think about yourself. Take the time, grieve and feel the pain, but then also let it go. Realize that you simply got too close to this person. Ultimately, he was afraid of being exposed by you and simply reflected his own problem onto you. Talk to friends about your feelings, ask for feedback from your loved ones about whether he was right in his accusations, and realize this: when you get honest feedback from the people you trust, there are very much people who love you. Don't be afraid to call the worry line (yes, that still exists) and/or contact a therapist. Your health insurance company can help you get a list. This pain, too, will pass. Realize that you will come out of this relationship stronger in the end.

But what if you yourself should decide to end this relationship? At this point, I can first congratulate you on your willpower. Very few women manage to get out of such a situation on their own. Often these relationships go on for many years. The women suffer silently, blame themselves exclusively and feel confirmed in their lack of self-esteem. When you finally decide to take this step, there are a few things to keep in mind.

You don't need to have empathic conversations with a narcissist; he won't admit his mistakes. Rather, he will play the ball back to you. Tell him succinctly that you no longer want the relationship, avoid giving reasons and thus painful discussions in which he reproaches you. Be prepared for him to be insulting, because the better he knows you, the better he can hit you where it hurts. And rest assured: he will hit you with everything he's got. Think about where you want the conversation to take place. I would advise against doing it in his apartment. A coffee shop can help "keep him in check" and create the necessary distance.

In the rarest of cases, he will take this "humiliation" in stride. This is where the term **"hoovering"** comes into play. This refers to a method he will use to "lull" you over and over again. The term comes from the English vacuum cleaner brand Hoover and means in a figurative sense that the ex-partner should be "sucked up" again. There are different forms of the approach:

- He constantly posts messages and/ or posts all over the social networks.
- There could be surprise visits on his part.
- You will always be reminded of the beautiful moments or shared experiences.
- He will suddenly realize all his wrongdoings and vow to mend his ways.
- He behaves as if nothing ever happened. This can go so far that he comes in and out of your house normally and may even continue to sleep next to you.
- He always finds occasions to get in touch with you.
- He demands his gifts back.
- He will not release your private belongings that are still in his possession.
- He talks about wanting to actively change, for example in the form of therapy.
- He appeals to your common sense, since after all they both suffer from the situation.
- Mutual friends are roped in to advocate for him.
- He can no longer live without you or even blames

serious illnesses and thereby tries to arouse your pity. This can even go as far as threatening suicide.

If you do not respond to these methods, he can vent his frustration through insults, fits of rage or even whole jealousy scenes. In the very worst case, the transition to stalking is not excluded.

Realize that these behaviors arise out of his rage to offend. For him, the priority is not to win you back because he really can't and doesn't want to live without you anymore, but rather the urge to bend you to his will and keep control. Even more - he wants to actively prevent you from building a happy and self-determined life. He simply wants to harm you. The problem is that this strategy is often not seen through or is misunderstood by his victim. As soon as you let yourself be "lulled" by his advances, assurances and romantic promises, this flatters his ego. After all, he is on the verge of controlling you again. As soon as he succeeds in doing this, he will quite quickly limit his blame shares: "I only did this because you ..." or "Maybe I made a mistake, but ...". Never will he take the blame for an obvious wrongdoing with all consequences, without ifs and buts.

Here only a total break off of contact can help!

And this is exactly what makes the separation so difficult for a dependent co-narcissist. For you as an empathic person, it is difficult to watch and endure that he suffers. The provocations are also difficult to endure because they are neither right nor fair and you feel the need to defend yourself against them. Take comfort: Deep down, he also knows that his accusations are nonsense. Should you keep responding to them, sooner or later you will buckle or experience a "neverending story". Your feelings are normal, after all, every breakup takes time and the one with a narcissist especially so. Realize that your longings are more like withdrawal symptoms. And these will pass with time.

YOU ARE NOT TO BLAME !

The most important thing first: do not blame yourself, because you are not to blame! Narcissists are very skillful and work extremely calculatingly and purposefully. It can happen to any of us! Through the methods of a narcissist described in advance, it should have become clear to you that such people work highly manipulative. A small life crisis is enough and it is easy for a narcissist to find fertile ground with you. Systematically you are driven into dependence and your fears are used against you.

However, if you have managed to get out of such a relationship, you should very well ask yourself what actually happened. Why did another person manage to gain control over your life to such an extent? How was it possible for you to ignore or tune out all the warning signs? It is important to deal with these questions intensively in order not to become a "repeat victim".

I would like to present to you below some of the reasons why you might have fallen for such a relationship:

Strength! Narcissistic men are self-confident, charming, appear strong and very well-groomed. Men with such a "standing" are most likely to appeal to women, because they know about your effect. For them it is not a big overcoming. For the rest of the male world, unfortunately, it is, so the chance is not insignificant that if a man addresses you, he may not be a narcissist directly, but it already speaks for his strong self-confidence. Of course, we women are flattered when a charming, strong man takes notice of us. Nevertheless - keep a cool head.

Spontaneity! Does he invite you to your favorite restaurant and you end up in his? Or would he like to have a coffee with you and you end up in a sex store together? Yes, you read correctly. This is probably a rather extreme example, but has actually already happened to me, if I may also mention a personal experience at this point for once. What can hardly be surpassed in audacity is for a narcissist an expression of relaxedness and spontaneity. If you confront him, you will probably hear that there is something wrong with you. You will quickly get a first bad conscience, after all, you want to be spontaneous and casual.

In truth, however, you will always be led around by the nose by him, disregarding your personal wishes and pursuing only his interests. Because he is certainly not spontaneous. If you are spontaneous, you might make mistakes. In fact, his restaurants and the sex store have always been his goals. Have confidence in yourself! Everything is right with you and how casual or spontaneous you are, after all, you still decide for yourself. If you like to eat Chinese, then insist on it and do not let yourself be led to the Italian without comment and under false promises.

Compliments! Let's be honest - each of us likes to hear them. But he also does not have to exaggerate. It is understandable that you would like to be recognized and loved. But realize that if you don't love yourself, no one else can do it for you.

Rollercoaster! The relationship with a narcissist makes you addicted. The mixture of different methods to make you jealous or keep you sometimes close, sometimes far away are highly emotional. Everything happens so fast that you can hardly keep up with getting yourself and your thoughts in order.

All your thoughts revolve around the question, "Does he still love me?" As you are fully occupied with being ready for him in case he ever calls again or taking care of him, friendships take a back seat. The hobbies that used to be so important to you suddenly aren't anymore. Of course, such behavior can also be observed at the beginning of a healthy relationship and is quite normal. The difference in this context, however, is that you do not feel safe, secure and accepted in a relationship with a narcissist, but rather stressed and rushed. Friends and hobbies are important to you. Especially when a difficult relationship goes to pieces, it is your friends who will catch you then and it is your hobbies that do you good and give you a positive self-esteem. Never neglect this.

Ultimately, it is very difficult (as mentioned earlier) to tell if you are dating a narcissistic man. Of course, not every man who approaches you is a narcissist. Maybe it also cost him an extreme amount of overcoming to approach you because he really likes you a lot. But stay alert. In today's fast-paced world, we are tempted to rush into relationships lightly.

The older we get, the greater the need to finally arrive at the One. We quickly get the impression that everyone around us has already arrived and you then wonder what is wrong with you personally. It could be, of course, that your standards are too high. This is a statement that every single person has heard from a girlfriend. But is it true? Demands change, sometimes they decrease, sometimes they increase and when the right person is standing in front of you, they don't matter anyway.

A healthy self-worth is poison for every narcissist

WHAT IS WRONG WITH ME AND OTHERS?

To be aware of oneself, to have confidence in one's own abilities and on the basis of this to look optimistically into one's own future describes a healthy degree of self-confidence. This "being convinced" of yourself and the confidence in your own person is ultimately also expressed in your appearance and is a key to success, both in professional and private terms.

In order to develop a healthy self-confidence, a certain degree of professional, social and personal appreciation is necessary. Each person derives more value from some areas and less from others. Men differ significantly from women in this respect. Whereas, statistically speaking, social recognition, good looks and independence through an income of one's own are most important for women, for men, finances and success at work are the top priorities.

The foundation for healthy development is laid in our childhood. However, many people are already given some inferiority complexes along the way in these early years of life. Educational deficits can be passed on in one direction or the other. Parents who attach above-average importance to their children's school grades can quickly give them the feeling that they never perform well enough and are not good enough, either for themselves or for others. These people will most likely have trouble developing a healthy level of confidence in their own abilities in adulthood. Conversely, many children today are taught by their parents not to put up with anything because they are always right.

At an early age, children begin to argue with teachers at school. Landing on the substitutes' bench in the club because they were often not at training or did not perform as they should is out of the question for their guardians. The children of these parents are always right. They will have problems in adulthood at the latest if, as a result of their parents' upbringing, they are unable, for example, to show any understanding for the criticism of their supervisor.

An "unhealthy" self-confidence can thus digress in both directions. It is not always easy to distinguish between a "real" and a "fake" self-esteem. In general, however, it can be said that people with an unhealthy self-esteem tend to be more conspicuous, while people with a genuine or healthy self-esteem are more inconspicuous and modest. To be able to tell this apart in real life, you need some practice and psychological background knowledge. However, in addition to building your own self-confidence, it is important to consider whether the behavior of those around you is "genuine" and whether these people deserve your trust.

Therefore, I would like to introduce you to some behaviors that a person with a healthy self-confidence simply does not do. Because behind such behaviors are often the very narcissists who have already made your life difficult many times - not only privately, but also professionally.

Attention is the most important thing for these people. They constantly seek praise and recognition in both their private and professional lives.

Envy and resentment are the predominant feelings. When something good happens to you, these people can quickly feel threatened by you. It's hard to tell if someone is honestly happy for you or not. Depending on the potential for danger you bring to the table, a covert grudge may change to an overt one. Confrontations or slights can then make life difficult for you.

I'm right. You've probably been to training courses or parties and thought to yourself: "There's always someone who knows everything better". These are the people who like to discuss a matter until even the last person has understood their point of view and is convinced of their opinion.

Me, me, me. A conversation can only work if there is a dialogue between at least two people. People with a false self-worth, however, prefer to hear themselves talk: their problems, their successes, and other people's misbehavior. They do not listen to other people, nor are they interested in whether they might also have problems.

Later. Also, people who are very creative in postponing any decisions and who just don't want to commit themselves show rather poor self-confidence.

Admiration for the achievements of others is

often commented on with "I could never do that."

Focusing on one's own weaknesses. No, this is not modesty, but testifies to the fact that this person should work on himself. They carry a negative self-image through the world and have the feeling that they consist only of shortcomings. This does not go unnoticed by others. As a result, the outside world also has little confidence in those affected. Professional success? Wrong! These people show little initiative and even after years sit in the same corner doing the same work.

Compliments? They can't handle that at all. Instead of being pleased and thanked, these people often reject compliments or feel directly in the position of having to make counterarguments. But not only do they have problems accepting compliments, they also automatically question their sincerity. Often, such people then feel "made fun of".

Confrontations? A foreign word for people with a lack of self-confidence. They can't judge when a discussion is appropriate and when they are in the right. In addition, they have a strong need for harmony and directly assume that their discussion opponent is superior and in the right anyway.

Finally, it is not only important to think about how

to interpret other people's behaviors, but also to think about what you need to work on. People with a false sense of self-worth or resulting narcissists, after all, have a particularly good nose for people with whom they can deal as they please. Even more: Narcissistically inclined people will even seek your closeness. Thus, it will automatically happen that you will meet such people again and again, even if you are not actively looking for a partner at all or try to be as inconspicuous as possible at work.

Therefore: A healthy self-worth is poison for every narcissist!

THEY ARE GREAT! - STRENGTHEN SELF-CONFIDENCE

If you internalize this sentence, then the most important step is done!

I would like to introduce you to some exercises below that can help you boost your self-confidence.

Exercise 1: Stand in front of the mirror, relaxed and as you do in everyday life. We often catch ourselves using a rather limp, contracted posture. This circumstance is often also due to a lack of physical activity.

Try to pull your shoulders back and push your chest forward a bit. For many, it is a rather unfamiliar posture. Nevertheless - try it out at your workplace, for example. You will quickly notice that this posture gives you more confidence.

Exercise 2: You probably have a mirror in your bathroom and also a lipstick. Paint a positive mantra on the mirror, for example the words "I am beautiful". Every time you enter your bathroom, you will read it and subconsciously memorize it.

Exercise 3: If you find yourself in an anxiety situation, it can help to take a short, conscious moment. Close your eyes, breathe in at one and out at two. Concentrate on your breathing and count to thirty in this way.

It is important that you try to regularly and frequently leave your comfort zone and do things that are difficult for you. For example, try taking a seat right up front in a university lecture or sitting close to the boss during a meeting at work. Get into the habit of this behavior and increase it. Just smile at a colleague as you pass by. I'm sure he or she will smile back.

You can also create success on your own. Consider joining a club or taking on a volunteer position. Doing something for other people makes you feel good. Since we often do not receive the recognition that is so important to us at work or often in our private lives, it is important to seek it elsewhere. Everyone is good at something, including you. Think about what that can be and then go for it. You can often find lists of sports clubs or volunteer activities on websites in your city.

Exercise 4: Silence your inner critic. To do this, you can get a bracelet whose top and bottom sides are different. Here, one side stands for praise and the other for criticism. Every time you catch yourself being critical of yourself, turn the bracelet around. Set small goals at first, such as an hour, then a day, a week, and so on.

Exercise 5: Maybe the time has come for an extended shopping trip, but you have no idea what suits you. In addition to professional type advice, you can simply ask someone who has a great style in your eyes. This does not necessarily have to be someone from your circle of friends. Just talk to your nice colleague. She will certainly help you. Because if you feel comfortable in your clothes, then you also radiate that.

Exercise 6: Get off the couch and out of the house. Go for a walk, swim or practice some other sport. Again, a club can help in this regard. Exercise is important. Especially in office jobs, this is unavoidable to maintain a healthy body image.

Exercise 7: Focus on problems, because there is a great danger of getting lost in you. Instead, look for ways to solve problems.

Exercise 8: Set small goals. It is important that these remain really small. It is better to set several small goals than to fail at large ones.

For example, a goal could be to exercise tomorrow, buy yourself flowers, take a bath, or clean out a closet. Feel free to write down all your goals for tomorrow in the evening and then check them off as well. It will do you good to remind yourself how much you actually get done.

On the Internet you will find heaps of exercises to increase your self-worth. And besides all the exercises, always make yourself aware that you are ok and your feelings and sensations are not aberrant. When you start to open up and maybe talk to people close to you,

you will realize that your emotions are not out of the ordinary and you have nothing to be ashamed of. On the contrary - most people are struggling with the same problems you are.

OVERCOME CRISES - PRESERVE HAPPINESS

To achieve a healthy self-confidence, it is important to activate your inner strength. This refers to our psychological power of resistance to face difficult life situations and every person possesses it since birth. This power of resistance, which is also called resilience, can be temporarily limited by various influences. Sudden crises or extraordinary stressful situations can be responsible for this.

In our example, this can be a narcissistic relationship with someone who convinces you that you are not right or the separation from your partner. In order for you not to be susceptible to such partnerships in the future, it is important to maintain your inner balance in addition to a healthy self-confidence. Especially for people who easily fall into dependent relationship structures or are prone to depressive episodes, it is essential to deal with this issue.

In this context, I would like to explain to you in more detail the model of the German psychologist Hilarion Petzold. According to this, our inner balance consists of five pillars. To find out what exactly disturbs your inner balance, it may help you to take a closer look at these pillars:

• Body and Health (Mental and Body)
• Social relationships (family, friends, neighbors, colleagues)
• Work and performance (recognition, sense of achievement)
• Material security (financial security, standard of living)
• Values and ideals (permissible, forbidden, rituals, morals)

Each individual pillar can be disturbed in very different ways. For example, the "body and health" pillar can be affected by your own dissatisfaction with regard to your physical fitness or illness.

Social relationships can be affected by separation, divorce or even a move to another city. It should be noted that while the individual pillars should basically be in balance, it is quite normal to place more value on one than the other. For example, it may be very important to you to have success in your career, but less important to be unable to maintain a certain standard of living. The important thing is that the other pillars provide a stable foundation and support when one begins to crumble.

If you feel that something in you is out of balance, three steps can help you regain your inner balance and return to your inner strength. The first step is about awareness. To do this, it makes sense to look at the five pillars described at the beginning of this article and ask yourself what situation is stressing you so much right now and why.

In a second step, the information phase, you deal with the topic of who or what can help you. Some of you may have already sought therapeutic help, but a counseling center may also be able to help you find suitable strategies for dealing with the difficult situation. Your own ideas can also be helpful here, for example finding out about new job offers if your job is too stressful, or considering joining a club if social friendly contacts are lacking after a move. In any case, it is only important that you honestly become aware of what is not going well for you at the moment, so that you can then take the third step to find the curve to action. Are you dissatisfied with your job? Then after the information comes the application. Often it is also quite good to test your "market value" and thereby get new motivation. Has stress led to health problems such as high blood pressure? Then exercise or relaxation techniques can help.

Mindfulness is the keyword here, and it applies to all areas of your life. In order to maintain your inner balance and strength, it is important to take a preventive approach to your own life in advance and not to take action only when you already notice that something is not right.

I would like to share with you some tips that will help you in this process.

1. Get to grips with your **body**. Listen to yourself and get a feeling for how you react to stress. How do they manifest themselves? Physically? Psychologically? There are different levels of stress. Each level also has an approach to relieving stress. For example, a slight inner tension after a stressful day can be relieved by aroma such as scented candles or oil.

Stronger tensions often have a physical access. In this case, it can be helpful to exercise or simply walk up and down the stairs several times. Which access you have for the respective degree of tension can be found out by testing. The more you deal with your body, the faster you are able to analyze where deficits in your well-being have just arisen and can also successfully rectify them.

2. A stable **social environment** is essential for your inner strength. As already described, it is important never to neglect your circle of friends or family connections. Because they are the ones you can confide in when your inner chaos threatens to take over.

3. Be aware of your **strengths** as well as your weaknesses and embrace both.

4. Schedule regular **"me" times when you** are the center of attention. It doesn't always have to be the extended wellness weekend. It's enough to snuggle up in your favorite chair with a book or soak in a bath. Even little things count and make you take yourself seriously.

5. Saying **no** is perfectly fine. Learn to listen to yourself and your gut and stand by your needs.

6. A **positive attitude to life** is the be-all and end-all. However, this sounds easier than it actually is. Nevertheless - don't try to see the negative in everything and/ or try to see something positive in supposedly negative things. After all, it is well known that the sun always comes out after the rain.

7. Pay conscious attention to the **good things** that happen to you in life, because we are often blind to them. The following applies: Even small good things are good. A little trick can help you. Put three marbles or coins in your pocket. Consciously pay attention to the small and big successes in your life. Every time you notice something, switch a marble or coin from your right pocket to your left pocket. If everything is on the left, then start again from the beginning. You will be amazed at how often this interplay can take place.

8. In addition to a positive attitude, a good **diet** is also essential. Drink plenty of water and little alcohol, also eat fresh and balanced. Because it is not for nothing that they say that in a healthy body lives a healthy mind.

9. **Sleep** is important to start a new day with fresh

energy. Make sure you have enough fresh air and good temperatures in your bedroom.

10. Despite all the good tips and sufficient preparation, it can still happen that a burden simply grows over your head. It is important to recognize this point, ask for **help** early on, and accept it when it is offered to you.

Often people with a rather negative self-image and low self-esteem have no sense of being important. But let me conclude by saying: If you don't dare to take yourself, your needs and burdens seriously and don't learn to do so, no one else will either!